Original title:
The Deep Sea's Voice

Copyright © 2025 Creative Arts Management OÜ
All rights reserved.

Author: Maxwell Donovan
ISBN HARDBACK: 978-1-80587-347-1
ISBN PAPERBACK: 978-1-80587-817-9

Serenade of Silenced Depths

In the abyss where fish wear hats,
Octopuses dance, like silly acrobats.
The crabs play poker, it's quite absurd,
With seaweed cards, and a blabbering bird.

A shark sings opera, but off-key,
While dolphins giggle, they think it's spree.
Bubbles burst with laughter all around,
Underwater glee is the silliest sound.

Secrets Carried by the Currents

Turtles gossip, sharing their tales,
Of mermaids with brushes and colorfulails.
Fish wear sunglasses, looking so cool,
As jellyfish float, just acting a fool.

Seahorses waltz in a clumsy way,
While starfish try to dance, but just lay.
The waves talk softly, with a tickle and tease,
Spreading giggles like a cool summer breeze.

Underwater Reflections: A Sonnet

A clam with a gram, posing with flair,
Winks at a crab, who just doesn't care.
Anemones wobble, pretending to walk,
Creating a scene that's quite hard to talk.

The turtles debate who's fashionably late,
While narwhals argue their points on a plate.
And fish in a school play charades for a thrill,
Each guessing the secret, with giggles to spill.

Songs of the Sea Creatures

In the blue depths, the bass fish groove,
Singing their songs with a slick little move.
The flounders flip-flop, trying to shine,
While the lobsters joke, 'We're doing just fine!'

Grouper and snapper, they take the stage,
Laughter erupts like a comical rage.
With bubbles of joy that float in the air,
The oceanic jamboree—beyond compare!

The Murmuring Depth

In ocean's belly, fish sing blues,
With bubbles popping, oh what a muse!
A crab plays drums on a clamshell stage,
While starfish dance, showing off their rage.

A whale cracks jokes, cracks us up, you see,
While octopi paint with ink so free!
The seaweed sways, it's quite the sight,
Underwater parties go on every night.

From Floor to Surface: Oceanic Echoes

The sea cucumber tells silly tales,
Of lost shipwrecks and jellyfish pales.
Sea anemones roll, giggling around,
Who knew such fun could be found unbound?

A dolphin splashes, it's quite a tease,
Making waves with absolute ease!
Crabs join the chatter, it's quite a show,
In this blue world, laughter does flow.

Tides of Emotion and Memory

Eels wiggle while gossiping fast,
About the clam who lost his cast.
Seahorses twirl in a silly ballet,
While hermit crabs wear homes like a play.

The water's filled with bubbles of glee,
As fish tell jokes, oh, it's wild, you see!
A turtle munches on seaweed delight,
Snapping selfies in the shimmering light.

Cascade of Whispering Fates

Do you hear the barnacles laugh and sing?
With sea lions joining as they swing.
A bottle-nosed friend tosses a ball,
While plankton forms a conga line call.

Coral reefs chuckle, they can't hold it in,
As schools of fish flash their best fin.
In the playful depths, all things are bright,
With laughter bouncing from day to night.

Beneath Storm's Tumult

Bubbles rise like giggles, a fish in a hat,
Seaweed dances funny, like a wiggly cat.
Shrimps are chattering secrets, in a bubble blow,
While crabs tell tall tales, in a clam shell show.

Octopus with eight arms, juggling seaweed,
Squirrels of the deep tide, can't find their feed.
A whale blows a trumpet, what a loud blast,
Fish shrug it off—'It's just Moby's fast!'

Songs of the Submerged

Dolphins in tuxedos, do the conga line,
Singing to the sea cows, sipping on brine.
Jellyfish with umbrellas, float like fine art,
Swirling in the currents, each playing a part.

Turtles wear spectacles, reading sea charts,
Seahorses gossiping about jellyfish arts.
A clam plays a piano, sharing a tune,
While shrimps form a choir, under the moon.

Cadence of the Ocean's Pulse

Waves crash like laughter, splashing the shores,
Starfish tap their toes, counting the scores.
A fish in a bowtie, winks as it glides,
While sea cucumbers wiggle, enjoying the ride.

Coral reefs are giggling, naptime's delight,
Crabs doing the shuffle, under starlit night.
Anemones dreaming, as bubbles float by,
And seagulls breakdance, beneath the open sky.

Each Drop Holds a Story

In droplets of laughter, secrets are spun,
Mollusks debate while they bask in the sun.
Waves play the games, where mermaids can cheer,
As fish make a splash, bringing party vibes near.

Barnacles gossip, super glued to their spot,
Clams snicker on jokes about what they forgot.
Each ripple a rumor, each tide a good jest,
Life under the surface is quite the wild fest!

Tales Exchanged in Silence

In the ocean's belly, fish wear hats,
Swapping secrets while dodging spats.
A crab narrates with a wiggly dance,
While starfish giggle, lost in their trance.

Octopus juggles pearls with grace,
While seahorses race, all over the place.
Anemones sway like they're feeling bold,
Telling tall tales of treasures untold.

But the whale, with a grin and a song,
Claims he's the coolest, the best all along.
With each splashy joke, waves break with glee,
In a deep-sea circus, just wait and see!

As bubbles bubble up with a cheer,
The stingrays join in, bringing up the rear.
Now who could have guessed that beneath the tides,
Are giggles and puns where laughter abides!

Murmuring Darkness of the Deeps

In shadows where the lanternfish flicker,
A pufferfish jokes, 'I'm no thicker!'
Clownfish chuckle, aware of the scene,
While eels do impressions of kings and queens.

A jellyfish floats, with a sway so bright,
As sea slugs plan their next silly fight.
With a wink and a nudge, they each take their turn,
Telling tales that make the seaweed churn.

The shrimp, with a pop, makes everyone laugh,
About the time he lost his own staff.
The corals roll their eyes and huff,
'We've heard this one plenty, enough is enough!'

Yet still they share jokes on the ocean floor,
Where squids tell tales, and laughter's in store.
So in the murk, where the dark currents weave,
Life winks and chuckles, what girls can achieve!

Rhythms of the Untamed Blue

In waters deep, the fish all dance,
With silly moves, they take a chance.
They shimmy and shake, with gills a-flap,
A wiggly waltz, who'd need a map?

Octopus stunts, he's full of flair,
Juggling seashells, without a care.
A whale comes in, adds his loud tune,
They laugh together, beneath the moon.

The Whispered Legends of the Ocean

The crabs hold court in a sandy seat,
Telling tall tales, oh what a feat!
With pincers raised, they jest and jibe,
Hypnotized fish, now join the tribe.

A starfish claims, he once was a star,
With shimmering lights, he traveled far.
But caught his glow in a net of goo,
Now he just watches, feeling blue.

Call of the Sirens in the Dark

The sirens sing, with giggles bright,
Their bubbles pop like fireworks at night.
"Come dance with us," they tease and flirt,
But fish all know, it's just dessert!

With goofy grins, they splash and play,
Trying to chase those tunes away.
For every note, a silly quirk,
The ocean's laugh is quite the work.

Untold Stories of the Ocean's Caress

A turtle tells of his race with speed,
But crabs just chuckle, "You're quite the breed!"
With shell on back and heart so bold,
He dreams of trophies made of gold.

The jellyfish floats like a balloon,
Stinging all things, "What a tune!"
Yet all just giggle at his plight,
For underwater jokes bring pure delight.

Deep Blue Reverberations

Bubbles giggle in the coral,
Shrimps dance like they're at a gala.
Octopuses swap the latest gossip,
While sea cucumbers just flop and loll.

Turtles wear shades, striking a pose,
While inkfish write with style, I suppose.
Clownfish joke, 'What's the deal with nets?'
As eel's puns leave everyone in sweats.

Melodies from the Ocean Floor

Sand dollars hum a little tune,
Crabs tap-dance beneath the moon.
Starfish sing with arms wide spread,
While jellyfish float in a groove instead.

Seaweed sways, it's quite the sight,
Flounders argue who's better at flight.
A lobster claims he's a chef divine,
But his cooking's just a crude line of brine.

Currents of Nostalgia

In the depths, memories flow like waves,
Fish reminisce of ancient caves.
Old conches chuckle at their own tales,
While plankton giggle in tiny sails.

Manta rays share their fashion tips,
"Don't be shy, let your colors flip!"
Anemones blush from too much sun,
While seahorses dance, just having fun.

Whales' Ballads beneath the Stars

Whales serenade in the starry night,
Their songs echo with such delight.
Dolphins flip like they own the stage,
While sea lions scribble on the page.

Fish quip, "What's a whale's favorite band?"
"Anything that makes them feel grand!"
Sharks snicker, "We're the cool ones here,"
But it's hard to hear over their own cheer.

Cool Depths

Bubbles giggle in the gloom,
Fish dance like they're in a room.
Octopus wears a fancy hat,
Waving fins, imagine that!

Jellyfish bounce like rubber balls,
Echoing laughter through the halls.
Dolphins tell the best of jokes,
While seaweed tickles sleepy folks.

Whispering Souls

Crabs in slippers, what a sight,
Shrimp doing pirouettes, oh so light.
Starfish giggle, spread out wide,
In this ocean, there's no pride.

Bubble-blowers, sea foam dreams,
Flopping fish with silly schemes.
Eels that wiggle, twist and twine,
In this world, it's all just fine.

Undercurrents of Emotion

A sea witch bubbling with delight,
Casts her spells, ignites the night.
Pufferfish in tiny clothes,
Prancing 'round, as everyone knows.

Sardines form a dance brigade,
Their flashy moves could start a parade.
Seahorses giggle, tickle and glide,
In this underworld, they've got pride.

Eclipsed by the Blue Veil

Mermaids sing with a fishy flair,
Tickling their tails without a care.
Sea turtles drop in for a wave,
Chasing shadows like a brave knave.

Anemones throw a grand ball,
Where no one worries at all.
Clownfish cracking jokes all night,
In this realm, there's pure delight.

The Sway of the Serene Waters

Corals laugh in vibrant hues,
Sharing secrets of the blues.
Lobsters strutting with swagger and pride,
Under the waves, they do not hide.

Oysters giggle, pearls in tow,
Tickling currents, making a show.
In this world, with humor rife,
Every splash brings joy to life.

Luminescent Dreams Below

In the darkness, fish hold light,
Dancing disco, what a sight!
Jellyfish twirl, a glowing plume,
Disco parties in the gloom.

Crabs in tuxedos, fancy prance,
Starfish join in, take a chance.
Seahorses spin like they're on stage,
Underwater, they share the rage.

Eels in velvet, lurking bold,
Telling tales of treasures told.
Anemones sway, they're quite the scene,
All together, a right marine dream.

Bubbles pop like tiny gongs,
Beneath the waves, they sing their songs.
Aquatic laughter fills the night,
In this ocean of pure delight.

Whalesong in D Minor

Whales hum tunes that make you sway,
In a melodic, clumsy way.
Bubble-blowers, whales on high,
They sing out loud, oh me, oh my!

Octopuses play the sax so smooth,
Dance a jig, make their move.
Tuna tap dance, fins all around,
Create a beat that's profoundly sound.

The krill join in with a little hum,
I think I even hear a drum!
While schools of fish form dazzling lines,
In this watery world, how everyone shines.

Underwater grooves, a vibrant show,
Making waves that ebb and flow.
In D minor, so offbeat and wild,
The party down here is so beguiled.

Phantoms of the Ocean's Heart

Ghostly shapes in the deep blue,
Whisper softly, Boo! Boo! Boo!
A playful shark in a ghostly cape,
Chasing shadows, what a shape!

Clowns in corals, clumsy as can be,
Making faces for the fish to see.
Squids play peek-a-boo with delight,
While dolphins dive, oh what a sight!

Mysterious bubbles rise and fall,
Echoing laughter, a ghostly call.
Specters twirl in the watery night,
In this realm, everything feels so light.

Their haunting giggles fill the sea,
Phantom parties, come join me!
With the tide's sway, they dance and dart,
In the hidden heart of the ocean's art.

The Language of Coral and Current

Corals chat in pastel hues,
Swapping secrets, sharing views.
They whisper soft, they giggle bright,
Under the waves, out of the sight.

The sea cucumber struts with flair,
Wiggling secrets beyond compare.
Urchins offer sharp advice,
While plankton dance, so sweet and nice.

Currents carry tales away,
Fishy gossip of the day.
Tides are turning, what a scene,
Waves splashing, it's all routine.

In this chatter, humor flows,
A sea of jokes that only ocean knows.
Listen closely, hear the jest,
In currents' laughter, we find our rest.

Murmurs of the Marianas

In the depths where bubbles pop,
Fish wear hats and never stop.
With laughter heard from coral reefs,
They tell jokes with fins like leaves.

Octopuses dance in a graceful sway,
While turtles waltz in a clumsy way.
They giggle as they flip and twirl,
In this underwater, silly world.

Crabs with crumpets munch and feast,
Having tea with a goofy beast.
In the shadows, a whale takes a nap,
Dreaming of his next fishy hap.

A starfish plays on a wobbly stool,
While seahorses whirl like they're in school.
Join the fun in this watery show,
Where every wave has a punchline to grow!

Voices Lost within the Tides

A clam is rhyming with a barnacle beat,
Making seaweed sway to a silly seat.
The tidal waves hum a groovy song,
While jellyfish jiggle, all night long.

Anemones giggle as the sea cucumbers stare,
In this world of laughter, none has a care.
Pufferfish puff, then let out a laugh,
As dolphins joke with their splashy graph.

The sea urchins grumble about their spiky fate,
Wishing for hugs instead of a plate.
While conchs chime in with a lyrical cheer,
Echoing fun for all sea creatures near.

A playful otter slips on a shell,
Creating a scene, oh, what a spell!
Dive in, join the bonkers tide,
Where every splash holds joy and pride!

A Symphony of Salinity

Harmonies bubble in salty air,
As crabs play maracas without a care.
Seashells chime with a ringing tone,
Driving fish crazy, all on their own.

Clownfish giggle, they know the tune,
As mermaids hum beneath the moon.
A conga line of squids slithers past,
Each doing the dance of the lunar blast.

The plankton whistle a bubbly refrain,
While sea turtles spin, never in vain.
In this concert, the octopuses shine,
With ink-blots and giggles, all in divine.

Every wave brings a chuckling sound,
In this rhythm, pure joy is found.
So waltz underwater, let laughter prevail,
In this oceanic, quirky tale!

Luminous Whispers of Distant Shores

Bioluminescent fish form a dazzling race,
Each lighting up like an underwater space.
They flicker and giggle, illuminating the night,
In this glow-in-the-dark aquatic delight.

Starry-eyed squids paint with their ink,
Creating masterpieces quicker than you think.
With each splash of color, they chuckle and grin,
Making art in the ocean, where fun won't thin.

A sandy bottom dance floor awaits,
Where flatfish boogie and never hesitate.
With a wink and a shimmy, they shimmy about,
While crabs clap their claws, cheering loud.

Seagulls swoop in to steal the show,
With a feathered fandango, a feathery flow.
Join the revels beneath the moon's rays,
Where every bubble brings smiles and plays!

Resonance in the Marine Abyss

In the depths where the bubbles hum,
A fish tells tales, but gets all dumb.
'Twas a sea cucumber, wearing a hat,
Claimed he had seen a long-lost flat.

Sharks with giggles, doing a dance,
Made other fish just want to prance.
They wore bow ties, bright as the spark,
Stealing the show, oh what a lark!

An octopus, juggling shells with ease,
Said, "Look at my skills, I'm quite the tease!"
With eight long limbs, he managed to fall,
Into a conch shell, blending with all.

In this blue world, the laughter's bright,
As creatures gather for a nighttime fright.
With every splash and a gurgled cheer,
Even the deep seems to have no fear.

Beneath the Foam: Oceanic Tales

Beneath the waves where the weird things dwell,
The squid plays poker, bets with a shell.
"He's bluffing!" cries out a sardine with glee,
While a whale sings ballads from a broken CD.

A crab in a tux struts with such flair,
As sea urchins giggle without a care.
"Do the cha-cha!" calls out a bouncy seal,
And suddenly, all join in with zeal.

They sip on kelp juice, quite the delight,
While a starfish spins tales that last all night.
A dolphin humms tunes from the top of his head,
In this underwater circus, none go to bed.

From the sand castle towers, they're all quite proud,
With seaweed flags waving in the crowd.
This realm is a party, laughter and fun,
Where every day feels like a mermaid's run.

Harmonies of the Coral Gardens

Coral reefs are bustling, what a show,
With fish on stilts putting on a toe-to-toe.
A clownfish clowns, tells the best joke,
While a blowfish puffs up in a cloak.

Turtles in sunglasses lounge in the sun,
Saying, "Life's a beach, and we're just having fun!"
Crabs play tag, moving sideways with flair,
While jellyfish float without a care.

Anemones wiggle, a dance party scene,
Spinning around like they're feeling serene.
The parrotfish squawks, "Come join my choir,
With bubbles and giggles, we'll reach for the higher!"

At the end of each day, when the moon starts to rise,
The sea creatures gather, sharing their lies.
For in this bright garden, laughter rings true,
Together they thrive, a wonderful crew.

The Language of the Dark Waters

In shadows where whispers roam and play,
A shrimp tells secrets, leading the way.
With nonsense rhymes and giggles galore,
While a moray eel just hides from the floor.

Fishes in fur confuse the wise mackerel,
"Is that a cat or a new kind of spectacle?"
A crab with a camera snaps silly poses,
As shoals gather 'round to share their noses.

Down where it's murky, surprises await,
An octopus twirls, declaring its fate.
"Who needs a hat when I have eight hands?
I'll juggle this clam, just to meet demands!"

As creatures of twilight share their deep bass,
The laughter rises, filling the space.
Each sound a story, each wave a dance,
In a world where the odd makes a joyful chance.

Hushed Halls of the Coral House

Within the coral's bustling halls,
Fish wear ties and have fishy brawls,
They gossip 'bout the tide's new style,
And laugh in bubbles, might stay awhile.

An octopus plays cards with clams,
While a clownfish jokes, just like he jams,
The seaweed sways to hidden tunes,
As crabs all shuffle, like dancing loons.

A starfish reads its latest tweet,
A turtle's slow dance is quite the feat,
The seahorses argue on who can twirl,
While jellyfish glow and frolic in swirl.

In the hush of blue, the laughter rings,
Each fin and tail knows how to sing,
Though all is quiet, watch the fun unfold,
In coral halls, where stories are told.

A Deluge of Untold Ballads

There's a whale who thinks he's quite the bard,
Shouting ballads, oh so avant-garde,
A fishy crowd gathers 'round in glee,
With sea turtles rug-cutting beneath the sea.

Anemones sway with every note,
While crabs tap dance in a tiny boat,
The sea cucumbers bob with might,
As the clam chorus hits a high note bright.

The anglerfish shines as a disco ball,
While shrimp take selfies, line up and sprawl,
They sing of currents, tales from the past,
In a world where fun is meant to last.

So listen close, there's music amid the waves,
Where even a grouper misbehaves,
In this underwater concert, the laughs will last,
A deluge of joy, in tales unsurpassed.

Beneath the Waves, A Resonant Heart

Beneath the waves where sea lives coo,
A puffer fish pops just to make you woo,
With a twirl and a spin, he goes for gold,
And his giggles spread, like secrets untold.

A dolphin's prank with a seaweed crown,
Has the whole reef laughing, spinning 'round,
Grouches hang back but can't help but grin,
When the merry clownfish busts a fin.

The jellyfish float with zany flair,
While sardines school up, a slippery pair,
Tales of ocean mischief echo wide,
In this sanctuary of laughter and pride.

Down in the blue, there's mischief afloat,
Where every creature dreams, dances, and wrote,
A resonant heart in the sea's vast play,
Beneath the waves, joy leads the way.

Celestial Conversations of the Deep

At night, the stars reflect in the tide,
As fish gather 'round for stories to bide,
An ancient turtle, wise and spry,
Shares tales of jellyfish who learned to fly.

A squid with ink makes his point clear,
While gobies giggle, "Oh dear, oh dear!"
They chat about mermaids and treasure near,
With dreams of swimming without any fear.

The colors collide in a wild parade,
As the deep whispers secrets, friendships made,
A seahorse speaks of its whimsical dress,
While sea stars applaud in shimmering finesse.

So tune in close; don't miss a beat,
In celestial talks, witty and sweet,
Under the waves, where laughter reigns,
The ocean narrates its playful domains.

Whispers Beneath the Waves

Bubbles giggle in the coral hue,
A clam named Cam talks to a shoe.
Fish in tuxedos do a dance,
While octopus juggles with great chance.

Crabs with sunglasses strut on by,
Their tiny claws waving hello, oh my!
Starfish play cards on the sandy floor,
While sea cucumbers snore and snore.

Jellyfish float like balloons in air,
Making silly shapes without a care.
Turtles race in slow-motion fun,
As dolphins pop up for a pun.

The seaweed wiggles, sways with glee,
As a whale sings loudly, "Look at me!"
Underwater laughter fills the blue,
Where even the kelp is laughing too.

Echoes from the Abyss

Down where the sun forgets to play,
A grouper tells tall tales each day.
A shark with shades gives fashion advice,
While plankton line up, oh so precise.

The blobfish, a creature of sheer delight,
Makes faces that give everyone fright.
Anglerfish flickers its lantern bright,
Saying, "Join my party, it'll be a fright!"

Anemones dance to the currents' tune,
While sea horses twirl under the moon.
With laughter and bubbles, they all engage,
In the ocean's wackiest, wildest stage.

A clownfish sets jokes to the sea flow,
While the mackerel dance to the show.
Echoes of chuckles fill every shell,
It's where the ocean loves to dwell!

Secrets of the Ocean Floor

Treasures hiding in the sand,
A forgotten flip-flop, isn't it grand?
The oyster has secrets, it won't tell,
While sea urchins giggle, oh so swell.

Tidal waves bring tidal jokes,
A dolphin snickers with coral folks.
While clams are making a stealthy bet,
The octopus messes with a tiny net.

Seahorses gossip, tails in a twist,
"Why did the fish cross? Let's find out, insist!"
The jellyfish float with a dreamy flair,
Wobbling around without a care.

The secrets here are brighter than gold,
Filled with laughter, a joy to behold.
Under the waves, where wonders soar,
A quirky party forever implore.

Murmurs in the Midnight Blue

In shadows where the moonlight dips,
Fish tell tales while doing flips.
A narwhal strums a seaweed harp,
As a grumpy old crab joins in, with a rasp.

Giant squids make dreadful faces,
While clam shells turn into party places.
The sea turtles boast, "We're the best!"
But the minnows know they're not like the rest.

Waves whisper secrets to the shadowed rocks,
Saving tales from trolls and flocks.
Underneath the starry dome,
The ocean laughs, its watery home.

With every ripple, a punchline flows,
As the moonlit tide universally glows.
Dive deep for giggles, it's a treasure hunt,
In the midnight blue, hilarity's front!

Rhythms of the Ocean Floor

The clams all dance with tiny feet,
Underwater, they skip to a beat.
Jellyfish jiggle with glee in the tide,
While sea cucumbers hide and abide.

Crabs throw a party, no napkins in sight,
With barnacles glued, they dance through the night.
Octopuses twirl in a colorful show,
While seaweed sways, like it's in a flow.

The fish have a laugh, they all throw a bash,
Sharing secrets in bubbles with a splash.
The squid pulls a prank, gives everyone fright,
With ink clouds of giggles dancing in twilight.

They sing underwater, so silly and proud,
The mermaids are laughing, a rowdy crowd.
As waves keep on rolling, they'll surely agree,
That fun can be found in the great salty sea.

The Silence that Roars

In the deep of the abyss, a whale takes a snooze,
His dreams full of fish, or maybe just blues.
Anemones chuckle at passing fish flies,
While a crab tells a joke that's full of good sighs.

Turtles wear sunglasses, they're cool and relaxed,
While sardines in formation, get frequently waxed.
A dolphin named Larry thinks he's on a roll,
He flips and he flops, but has lost his control.

Blowfish in style, puffed up with a grin,
Chorus of corals that invite them to join in.
Seahorses giggle, tied up in their strings,
With that kind of laughter, who needs diamond rings?

So listen closely, beneath all that blue,
You'll hear all the laughter, vivid and true.
For though it seems quiet, a party's in play,
In quirky, deep waters where the funny fish sway.

Mysteries of the Blue

Bubbles rise high, what a funny parade,
A lobster in tights, now that's a charade!
Clownfish keep cracking their jokes all around,
While sea stars are told to stand firm on the ground.

The anglerfish grins, with a lamp on his head,
"I'm lighting the way for the party ahead!"
Nudibranchs prance in their colorful suits,
While oysters gossip, and don't care for roots.

The sea floor is lively, livelier than streets,
With conch shells that blare out some funky beats.
Bubble-blowers practicing deep-diving tricks,
Making quite the spectacle, a laughter mix.

In this world underwater, who knows what you'll find?
Echoes of laughter leave worries behind.
So dive in for treasures, both silly and bright,
For mysteries hide where the sea is alight.

Hidden Harmonies of the Atlantic

In Atlantic's embrace, a concert is heard,
Where surfboards of dolphins and seals upturned.
Musicians of nature, the whales sing in tune,
While clowns of the seabed dance under the moon.

The shrimp write their symphonies as bubbles they blow,
And the turtles clap slowly, oh what a show!
With each little splash, a new verse is born,
As the laughter of krill fills the ocean with scorn.

Anemones sway with a sway like ballet,
While the octopus winks in a playful display.
Frogs in the ivy croak rhythm and rhyme,
While fish jam together, beats keeping time.

As currents all blend in their watery flow,
The wonders of rhythm continue to grow.
So if you feel lucky, don't forget to dive,
In this symphony deep where laughter's alive!

Underwater Requiem

Bubbles float with a giggle,
Fish dance in a wiggly wiggle.
A crab with a hat, how absurd!
He struts like he's having a word.

The octopus juggles a shell,
While seaweed twirls, casting a spell.
A turtle sneezes and causes a splash,
With laughter that echoes, oh what a bash!

The jellyfish glows in hues bright,
As clams tell jokes with delight.
Anemones sway to the beat,
In this watery world, life's a treat.

So, dive down below, don't be shy,
Where silliness swims, oh my oh my!
Each creature with quirks, a sight to see,
Under the waves, it's fun and free.

Ballad of the Bioluminescence

In the dark where the flashes appear,
Creatures giggle in tones sincere.
A fish dons a glow-in-the-dark tie,
While squids paint the night with a sigh.

The plankton sparkles like stars on the sea,
"Oh look at me, I'm a light-up marquee!"
A dolphin dances, all spruced up,
With a shimmer that says, "Come join the cup!"

The deep friends unite in a glowing parade,
With laughter and tail swishes they've made.
In this canvas of bubbles, enjoy the show,
Undersea antics, they steal the glow!

So join in the fun, don't miss the sight,
Where color and comedy light up the night.
In the whimsical waves, let your spirit take flight,
For the depths hold laughter, so perfectly bright.

Depths of the Ancient Abyss

In caverns deep, where shadows play,
An eel tells tales that never sway.
With sage-like wisdom and a wink,
He collects thoughts in a kraken's ink.

The turtle, wise in his old age,
Tells jokes that could fill up a page.
"I once lost my shell," he starts with a grin,
"Then found it again, two sizes thin!"

The anglerfish flicks on his light,
"Who needs a date? I'm quite alright!"
He winks at the sharks, who roll their eyes,
"Not your type, buddy, we're way too wise!"

In this ancient hole, fun never quits,
With each creature's charm, they break into fits.
So dive on down, don your best cheer,
Where the depths of wisdom are filled with a sneer!

Sonorous Currents of the Deep

In swirls and twirls, the currents sway,
Fish whistle tunes as they play.
A grouper hums in a jazzy beat,
With crustaceans tapping their tiny feet.

The sea anemone throws a rave,
While pufferfish puff up and behave.
"Let's dance in the dark," a clownfish calls,
While starfish spin on their sticky walls.

A mermaid croons with laughter loud,
Her scales shimmer bright, she's quite proud.
"Join in my song, let's swim and twirl,
In the depths we'll frolic and swirl!"

So dive with glee and join the refrain,
Where jokes and songs flow like the rain.
In the currents of joy, let laughter leap,
For beneath the waves, the fun runs deep.

Beneath the Stars 'Neath Starlit Waters

Bubbles rise, a fizzy dance,
A fish slips by in a little prance.
Octopus winks, tentacles twirl,
"Hey there, buddy, come on, let's swirl!"

Seaweed tickles a dandy crab,
Who struts his stuff, looking fab.
A starfish claps in its own way,
Who knew they'd party at the bay?

Jellyfish glow like floating lamps,
Lighting up schools of sleepy champs.
Sharks spin tales of old sea fights,
While dolphins giggle at their bites.

Under the moon, they all unite,
A raucous crew, what a delight!
Beneath the stars, they laugh and play,
Who needs a stage with such a sway?

Songs of Lost Navigators

Sailors once lost in the deep blue,
Now sing sea shanties, oh so askew.
"I thought I saw land, but it was a whale!"
"No, that was just a giant scale!"

Maps are tossed, tossed far and wide,
As fishfolk giggle, they take great pride.
"North or south? Well, who can tell?"
"Just follow the bubbles, they ring like a bell!"

Kraken snickers in his dark nook,
As sailors chase shadows from a book.
"The compass spins, must be magic!"
Nope, just more jokes – how tragic!

Yet laughter echoes through ocean's might,
From morn to moon, they sing of plight.
With every stumble, every wrong course,
The sea sings back with a chuckling force!

Chants of the Abyssal Wanderers

Down in the deep where shadows play,
The wanderers sing at the end of the day.
A squid draws sketches in the mud,
Crafting jelly beans that never flood.

A grouchy fish with a glittery crown,
Says, "Life's a joke, but I won't frown!"
Anemones giggle, tickling fins,
As clams and shells join in on the spins.

Giant squids tell tales of their fights,
But they're just tales of glow-stick nights.
"Who needs a sword when you flash and gleam?"
In dazzling colors of a dream.

So let the currents hum and sway,
While the wanderers charm the night away.
With laughter bubbling, hearts are free,
Dancing casually 'neath waves of glee.

Currents Carrying Time's Song

Currents gurgle, in a funny tone,
As clowns of the reef perform alone.
A sea cucumber sings with flair,
While turtles join in, without a care.

Time flows slick like a fishy sigh,
As giggles echo from the fishes' eye.
"If we could only catch a break!"
The octopus muses, "For goodness' sake!"

Coral cheeks blush in brilliant hues,
As whispers dance on the salty blues.
"Why was the crab so crusty, you ask?"
"Because he couldn't find his favorite task!"

So let the waters weave their song,
With every splash, they hum along.
In time's embrace, they twist and twirl,
As bubbles pop and laughter swirls!

Reverberations of the Hollow Deep

In the ocean's belly, a grumpy whale,
Tells fishy jokes that always fail.
Crabs wear glasses, think they're profound,
But ticklish jellyfish swim all around.

Starfish gossip, swapping finny tales,
While seahorses dance, wearing tiny veils.
A clam tries stand-up, but just can't find
The punchline hidden in shells behind.

A shrimp conducts, with a spatula long,
While dolphins join in, harmonizing wrong.
Octopuses juggle, misplacing their loot,
And everyone chuckles at the silly pursuit.

The deep has laughter, bubbling and bright,
With creatures that jest in the shimmering light.
So dive down below for a giggle or two,
In the merry depths, there's always a view!

Whispers from the Abyss

In the shadows deep, a flounder grins,
Telling up-boat stories about where he's been.
Fish on a coffee break share a latte,
With bubbles of laughter—such a fishy café!

A grouper wears socks that are polka-dot,
Says, 'Have you seen a fish in a yacht?'
Crustaceans debate who's the best at hide and seek,
While anemones giggle, tweaked by a peek.

An eel, with swagger, shows off his dance,
While a school of sardines hooks up for romance.
The ocean's a stage with a bumpy old floor,
Where performers are fish—we just need more!

Bubbles of humor swim all around,
In the valleys where silly fish are found.
So listen closely, beneath the sea's bed,
For laughter and joy that can always be spread!

Echoes Beneath the Waves

Beneath the waves, a clownfish jests,
With tiny puns that nobody protests.
A dolphin's quick with a witty remark,
While sea cucumbers hide in the dark.

Squids play charades in a tangled ballet,
While sea turtles joke at the end of the day.
The octopi giggle in multiple ways,
Sharing their secrets in clever displays.

A stingray drags in an awkward slapstick,
As iridescent fish aim for a quick kick.
With bubbles of joy, they all intertwine,
In the playful depths where the sun tends to shine.

So come take a plunge and join in the fun,
With creatures that sparkle when day is done.
In the vibrant expanse of the salty blue,
There's laughter galore just waiting for you!

Murmurs of the Ocean's Heart

In the murky deep, where the currents yawn,
A pufferfish bursts, just to carry on.
Gobies tell tales, the silliest lore,
While nudibranchs prance on the sandy floor.

Sponges wear hats, attend a grand ball,
Where barnacles dance, but can't stand tall.
A starry night in the water so deep,
With playful whispers that bubble and leap.

A bonito strapped in a tutu bright,
Swims past a sea urchin, what a fright!
Everyone chuckles, can't help but grin,
Even the corals join in on the din.

So if you decide to explore the waves,
Remember the whispers of joyful braves.
For laughter and fun whirl all around,
In the vibrant place where the silly abound!

Shadows of the Sunken Realm

In the deep where the fish wear hats,
The crabs all dance and gossip like bats.
A mermaid's laugh, a bubble each time,
Makes everyone giggle in water's rhyme.

An octopus juggles glowing pearls,
While starfish prance in swirly swirls.
The jellyfish, well, they float with flair,
Acting like floaty, wobbly air!

Tales of the Tides

Once a whale slipped on a slippery eel,
With a splash and a giggle, it was quite the deal!
The dolphin laughed, oh what a show,
As the sea turtle rolled with a giggling glow.

The waves told tales of silly fish fights,
With angler lights and flashing sights.
They slapped their fins and shared silly quirks,
While clams held secrets, buried in lurks!

Serenade of the Sirens

The sirens sing in a cackling tone,
Enchanting sailors with a rhythm of bone.
But instead of doom, they tickle instead,
With seaweed confetti that's splashed on your head.

They pull strange pranks on boats passing by,
Like swapping the compass to please a shy guy.
With each swoop and sway, they dance through the spray,

Spreading giggles where fish like to play!

The Call of Kraken's Lair

Down in the deep where the kraken plays,
He spends his time in amusing ways.
With eight squishy arms, he throws giant pies,
And watches as sailors get hit by the flies.

He calls to the gulls with a gurgling cheer,
"Come taste my cake, it's surprisingly dear!"
But if they decline, oh what a fuss,
He'll tickle their bellies and turn it to dust!

Celestial Chorus of Deep Waters

Bubbles pop like tiny stars,
Fish play tunes on guitar bars.
Jellyfish dance in a wiggly sway,
Who knew they could party all day?

Octopuses juggle with eight tiny arms,
Mermaids giggle, flaunt their charms.
A crab DJ spins shells on the floor,
While seahorses glide by, what a score!

The eel does a twist, then a shimmy,
While plankton laugh, feeling quite zippy.
Turtles tap-dance with some flair,
In this underwater concert fair!

So grab your fins, join the fun,
In the sea, we've only begun.
The ocean hums a silly song,
Dance with us; you can't go wrong!

The Riddle of the Roiling Waves

What's the thing that tickles the beach?
The waves whisper secrets, if you care to reach.
They laugh as they splat, tumble, and roar,
'Why did the fish cross? To get to the shore!'

Seagulls squawk their riddle each day,
'Why don't fish ever play the banjo?' they say.
The waves giggle back, 'Because they can't hold!
Their fins are too slippery, or so I'm told!'

A crab claps claws, joins in the jest,
While dolphins flip, performing their best.
'This ocean's a puzzle, full of fun lore,
With mysteries deeper than the ocean floor!'

So heed the waves, their laughter is bright,
For beneath their frolic, there's always delight.
In the puzzling tides, let silliness flow,
As humor weaves through the ebb and the flow!

Lament of the Lonesome Mariner

A lonesome sailor, out on the brine,
Complains to the fish, 'Can you spare me a line?'
But the fish just float, their gills all agog,
'Your boat's not a karaoke, don't be such a slog!'

The seagull scolds him, 'Quit your sad song!
You're sailing with fish—sweeten it up, not prolong!'
The waves chuckle softly, 'What's your crisis?
Leave the blues behind; life's a grand slice!'

He casts out his rod, but it catches a shoe,
And the fish in the sea laugh, 'What else can he do?'
He sighs and drinks sea spray, thinks, 'What a joke,
I'm the punchline here, and I'm just a bloke!'

So if you sail alone on the crest of the sea,
Remember the laughter; it's wild and free.
For even a mariner, stuck all alone,
Can find humor hidden in every groan!

Beneath the Hull: Songs Unseen

Under the hull, where the shadows play,
A party of critters holds court every day.
They bop to the rhythm of the waves' sweet hum,
While barnacles tap their feet in a drum!

The fish fry popcorn; it pops just for fun,
As a clam croons softly, 'Why so glum?'
A crab be-bops to his own little beat,
With jellyfish glowing, bringing the heat!

The octopus conducts this quirky parade,
In a symphony formed of seaweed and shade.
Whales join the chorus, but theirs is a blare,
And the fishes all giggle, 'Too much breath to spare!'

So if you ever glance at the sea's gentle roll,
Know beneath the surface, there's fun on a stroll.
For laughter is hidden in currents and swells,
In the songs of the ocean, where happiness dwells!

Echoing Shadows of the Sea

In the abyss where fish sing loud,
A crab tells jokes to a passing cloud.
The octopus juggles seashells with glee,
While a dolphin rehearses its stand-up spree.

The starfish pretends it's a disco ball,
As jellyfish dance to a bubblegum call.
With laughter bubbling up to the shore,
Each creature is wishing for just a bit more.

A whale and a shrimp have a comedy show,
With punchlines that come from the ocean's flow.
They splash and they squirt, what a sight to see,
While a sea turtle nods, "This is life's spree."

In the deep shades of blue, fun never ends,
With giggles and guffaws, the current bends.
So next time you dive, wear a smile wide,
For beneath the waves, the nonsense won't hide.

Ocean's Ancient Anthem

The clams form a band, what a strange sight,
With sounds very off, though they play with delight.
A seal steals the show, with its clumsy ballet,
Rolling and flopping in a comical way.

The sea cucumbers groove on the floor,
While bubbles erupt and they beg for an encore.
A fish with a hat cracks a pun so divine,
As seagulls tune in, drinking oceanic wine.

Old turtles spill tales of fresh-water falls,
While the deep ocean floor gets wobbly calls.
The crustaceans gather to share all the jokes,
Echoing laughter from all of the folks.

So heed the weird songs from the watery crew,
Where each serenade comes with a splash or two.
In rhythms and giggles, the waves sway along,
A concert of chaos, the sea's goofy song.

Unheard Symphonies of the Deep

Beneath the waves where the weird things thrive,
A clam tries to rap, but it barely survives.
The seaweed sways to an offbeat groove,
While silly sea horses attempt to improve.

Fish wear top hats in a fancy parade,
As they dance through the reefs, unafraid.
Anemones cheer with their tentacles wide,
Their roars of laughter flow with the tide.

An old lobster spreads gossip, it's quite a spiel,
While shrimp shake their tails, full of zeal.
A conch sings opera, though it's quite shrill,
In the vibrant abyss, the quirks give a thrill.

The currents hum tunes from ages before,
Where humor and chaos meet on the floor.
In the depths so dark, fun is the key,
Unlocking the laughter from deep in the sea.

Inky Depths of Hidden Dreams

Quietly lurking in the shadowy gloom,
Squid throw a party in their inky room.
They whirl and they twirl, painting canvases bright,
As the fish become brushes, oh what a sight!

A shy little shrimp, with dreams of being grand,
Doodles its hopes in the soft ocean sand.
While sea urchins giggle, just having their fun,
They chant silly rhymes in a chorus, well done.

With treasure maps scrawled in squiggly lines,
Starfish chuckle at mermaid designs.
The dolphins dive down to add to the scene,
Joining the fest with their jumps so serene.

The laughter rolls deep like the tides of the night,
Where dreams and deep thoughts take glorious flight.
So remember, my friend, if you skim the blue,
The sea holds a humor, just waiting for you.

Voices of the Forgotten Depths

Bubbles rise like giggles in waves,
Silly fish hold secret raves.
Octopus spins in disco lights,
Dancing clams enjoy their nights.

Jellyfish float like balloons in air,
With every drift, they spread their flair.
Crabs debate the best dance move,
While seaweed sways to their groove.

A whale sings jokes in echoing tones,
Making rockfish laugh with their groans.
Creatures in rows play musical chairs,
Each one grinning, with wavy glares.

In coral gardens, laughter blooms,
Snapper crack jokes in shady rooms.
Together they twirl in the moon's glow,
Who knew the ocean could put on such a show?

Lullabies of the Mariana

In the abyss where shadows play,
Starfish snore in a lazy way.
Squid serenade as they glide,
With bubbles as their melody guide.

Crustaceans rock in seabed cribs,
Counting plankton instead of fibs.
Seahorses sway in dreamy trance,
Hoping for a midnight dance.

The lanternfish glow like bedtime lamps,
While sleepy turtles, oh how they stamp!
A sleepy surge, the waves hush low,
As sleepy seals find their flow.

In tides that turn to gentle sighs,
Giggles mingle with sleepy cries.
With lullabies drifting through the blue,
The night wraps up in a watery hue.

Songs in the Silence

In silence, fish hum their own tune,
Cuckoo clams clap under the moon.
A shipwreck's echo sings stories old,
As sea cucumbers gather, brave and bold.

Brushing past anemones, they swear they dance,
With each gentle wave, they take a chance.
Moray eels chuckle, making jokes,
While deep-sea vents release puffs of smokes.

The deep may be dark, but laughter's found,
In the pitch-black waters, joy abounds.
A grouper croons with rhythm so sweet,
While anemones sway to the ocean's beat.

Every silence hides a giggling spark,
Echoes of mirth in the ocean's dark.
Deep tales unfold with each bubble blown,
Creating a symphony of cheer alone.

Conversations with Nautilus

Nautilus spins in his cosmic shell,
Whispering secrets of ocean dwell.
"Did you hear the jellyfish's latest hit?"
"I wrote the tune, isn't it a bit?"

Crusty crustaceans nod in delight,
"Can we dance to that tune tonight?"
Anemones giggle as they sway,
"Count us in for a lively display!"

The nautilus shrieks, "This party's swell!"
As they all dive into a jellyfish spell.
"We'll twirl 'til dawn, then float away,
Under sea moons, we'll laugh and play!"

With shells and fins, they spin 'round tight,
Creating whirlpools of pure delight.
In the ocean's core, they lift their voice,
Together they laugh; oh, what a choice!

Lanterns of the Abyss

In dark waters glow jellyfish bright,
They dance with grace, what a silly sight!
A ballet of bulbs in a cosmic jam,
Who knew that squishy things could be glam?

The fish all giggle, with scales that shine,
"Who paid for the glow?" "You? Oh, it's fine!"
With bubbles like laughter, they twirl around,
In this wacky world, joy is profound.

A turtle plays sax, with seaweed notes,
While crabs join in, in tiny coats.
Each wave is a chuckle, each splash a grin,
In this underwater show, let the fun begin!

So come join the party, no need to disguise,
Where lanterns of laughter light up the skies.
With fins and flippers, we all unite,
Undersea giggles, what sheer delight!

A Realm of Harmonious Silence

Bubbles float softly, like whispers of glee,
In a realm where even fish sip their tea.
An octopus plays chess, oh what a tease,
While starfish cheer in a chorus of wheeze.

A clam tells jokes tucked inside its shell,
"Why did the seaweed start its own tale?"
"Because it could not stop, it was fully engaged,
In a comedy routine that never aged!"

Coral reefs chuckle, so colorful and loud,
Holding meetings where no one's allowed.
"Shh! It's a secret, don't tell the waves!
We're plotting a dance to celebrate caves!"

So float in the silence, hear the laughter rise,
As fish share their secrets beneath the blue skies.
In this realm of fun, there's no need to shout,
Just swim with the flow, let your joy take route!

The Ocean's Unwritten Epic

A whale starts to rhyme in the water so blue,
With witty verses just sticking like glue.
He calls all his buddies to join in the fun,
While dolphins play flutes, oh what a run!

An anglerfish sings, "Where's my spotlight?"
With a lure that flashes, it's quite a sight!
"Don't crowd me, folks, I need my own space!"
Said the fish in despair, with a comical face.

A crab takes the lead with a tap dance so slick,
While seahorses follow—oh, what a trick!
Each wave a new page in their frolicking tale,
An epic of giggles where none can fail.

So join in the merriment, splash all about,
In this oceanic saga, there's no doubt.
With tides of humor, the sea tells its lore,
An unwritten epic forever in store!

Language of the Tidal Giants

In the glow of the tides, the giants convene,
With whispers of laughter, absolutely benign.
Their bubbles create words that tickle the ear,
In a dialect cheery, all giggles and cheer.

The kraken who juggles his treasures galore,
"Catch me a fish!" he calls out to the shore.
While octopus poets spill ink from their hearts,
As laughter erupts in the grinning sea arts.

Giant clams hold court, with pearls of great wisdom,
"Life's too short! Join our rhythm!"
Squidding is easy, just wiggle and squirm,
You'll find that it's fun; don't be so firm!

In these depths of humor, friendships are made,
With waves of delight that will never fade.
So listen closely; the giants proclaim,
A language of joy that will never wane!

Beneath the Surface: A Ballad

Bubbles rising, fish do dance,
A clownfish lost in a silly prance.
Octopus painting with polka dots,
While sharks wear ties and look quite hot.

Jellyfish glow like disco lights,
They boogie down through starry nights.
A sea turtle says, "I'll take my time!"
And crabs just snap in perfect rhyme.

The anglerfish holds a lamp so bright,
Waving it round, giving quite a fright.
The flounder plays hide-and-seek,
While a blowfish puffs up, feeling chic!

In this world beneath the waves,
Everyone dances, no need to save.
So join the fun where laughter's free,
In a splashy ballad beneath the sea.

Poetry of the Pelagic

In ocean's depths, where bubbles talk,
A whale sings softly while dolphins mock.
Crabs wear hats, thinking they're grand,
While sea urchins giggle, taking a stand.

Seahorses horse around in a race,
With sparkling scales, they keep their pace.
And jellys jiggle with jelly-filled glee,
Making waves that tickle the knee.

The sardines swirl like a scrumptious dish,
While starfish make a very bold wish.
They dream of a beach where they can lay,
But tide pools laugh at their silly play.

In underwater realms, joy reigns supreme,
Where fish float lightly, chasing their dream.
Join the laughter, let worries flee,
With the pelagic poets of the sea.

The Siren's Call

Oh, mermaids sing with hair so bright,
Luring sailors on a moonlit night.
But with a wink, they dive away,
Leaving the crew to dance and sway.

A kraken plays cards with feathery squid,
Trying to bluff, oh what a kid!
The seaweed twirls in a green ballet,
While fish root for their fave seafood play.

Giant clams hold pearls in their grip,
Pretending to be a fabulous ship.
They shout, "Avast! Thieves are near!"
But who would steal just to save a leer?

Under the waves, in waters so vast,
The laughter echoes, a joyful blast.
So heed the call, let spirits steer,
For the jokes of the ocean are always near!

Ballads of the Midnight Zone

In depths where sunlight fades away,
Creatures glow like stars in play.
A fish with glasses reads a book,
While a squid gives each tentacle a look.

Turtle races a jelly on a stroll,
While crabs on scooters roll on a pole.
A submarine squeaks, wishing it could dive,
While plankton wink and come alive.

Whales boast tales of deep-sea dreams,
Their laughter bubbles through silent streams.
Anglerfish grins with bait on the line,
Saying, "Dinner's ready at half-past wine!"

So come down deep where the fun's refined,
In the midnight zone, joy intertwined.
With ballads sung by the ocean's crew,
Life's a fishy joke meant just for you!

Secrets of the Submarine Silence

Bubbles bubble, fishy giggles,
Eels tell jokes, while seaweed wiggles.
Crustaceans dance, with shells in a whirl,
As jellyfish float, giving twirls and swirls.

Octopus chefs in culinary quest,
Whip up delights, it's a tasty fest.
Shrimp play maracas with clacking claws,
While clownfish chuckle, breaking the laws.

Beyond the waves, the sardines prance,
In slippery suits, they lead a dance.
Seashells echo, secrets they keep,
While snails wear hats, in a party deep.

So if you think the ocean's a bore,
Just listen close, there's laughter in store.
For beneath the calm, with humor untold,
The deep is alive, with treasures of gold.

Lullabies from the Blue Depths

Whales croon softly, in a melodic hum,
With dolphins joining in, oh, what fun!
Sea cucumbers sway, in peaceful serenade,
While manta rays glide in a rhythmic parade.

Coral reefs chuckle at the clownfish's pranks,
As sea turtles waddle, with some awkward thanks.
Starfish applaud with their five busy arms,
For the shenanigans, that have their charms.

Anglerfish flicker, lighting the night,
While grumpy old crabs just grumble and bite.
But if you catch their gaze, they might crack a smile,
And join in the lullabies for a while.

The ocean rocks gently, in harmonious cheer,
Under the surface, the laughter is clear.
In this watery nursery, dreams take their flight,
As the tide hums softly, through day and night.

Songs of the Sunken Souls

Ghostly shipwrecks share their tales,
Of treasure hunts, and sailor fails.
Mermaids giggle, tossing seaweed crowns,
While ship rats scamper, in anchor towns.

Crab choirs sing about their lost mates,
While silverfish wiggle, swaying in crates.
Barnacles hum in this joyful refrain,
As sea anemones dance, free of disdain.

Seahorses prance like a parade of style,
In tiny tuxedos, they strut for a while.
The old octopus plays a watery tune,
As the sunbeams dance through the waves of the moon.

Collective giggles echo from the wreck,
As fishy souls sing, without any check.
In these depths where laughter bubbles and swirls,
The songs of the sunken continue, like pearls.

Tides of the Forgotten

Sea urchins whisper secrets of lore,
While starfish plot, of pranks to explore.
The tides roll in with a chuckle and cheer,
For laughter's a treasure that's always near.

Forgotten ships weave tales in the sand,
With barnacles spotting each rusted hand.
Nautical nonsense fills every nook,
As eels tell stories from a well-worn book.

The ocean is silly, a playful expanse,
As plankton twirl in a whimsical dance.
Old seaweed boasts of adventures so grand,
While waves giggle softly, hand in sandy hand.

So listen closely next time you wade,
The tides of the forgotten have laughter displayed.
In this watery world, where humor's the prize,
The sea sings sweetly, beneath the blue skies.

www.ingramcontent.com/pod-product-compliance
Lightning Source LLC
Chambersburg PA
CBHW060127230426
43661CB00003B/355